Contents

1	Introduction	4
2	Political censorship	8
3	The power of the owners	14
4	Censorship and war	17
5	Religion and blasphemy	22
6	Obscenity	27
7	Film and TV censorship	33
8	Libel and the right to reply	38
9	Censorship in context	42
Glossary		46
Further reading		46
Further information		47
Index		48

Introduction

> When I was shot in the doorway of my North Belfast home in May 1984 I had no idea what organization the gunmen were from - they could have been from one of five death squads which had threatened my life during the past decade. As I lay there, the gunman stepped over me and went to shoot me in the head but the gun jammed and simply clicked two or three times. (Jim Campbell, *Index on Censorship.*)

The Northern Ireland journalist saved by a jammed gun in that incident backs up the playwright George Bernard Shaw's comment on censorship. Shaw said that the ultimate form of censorship is assassination, by which he meant that it is the best way of ensuring that the victim is never heard from again.

A narrower and more widely accepted definition of censorship is that it involves the control of information that is given out. Any restriction on the right to freedom of expression can also be viewed as censorship. The word itself is often used as a term of abuse and implies a feeling of restriction, of limitation of freedom and of preventing people doing what they want to do and saying what they want to say.

In recent years so-called death sentences have been passed on writers whose work is considered offensive, among them Salman Rushdie. It is an effective way of censoring them.

Points of
VIEW

·C·E·N·S·O·R·S·H·I·P·

Christian Wolmar

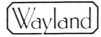

Wayland

Points of View

Abortion
Advertising
Alcohol
Animal Rights
Crime and Punishment
Censorship
Divorce
Drugs

Medical Ethics
Northern Ireland
Nuclear Weapons
Racism
Sex and Sexuality
Smoking
Terrorism

Front cover: *A policeman prevents reporters from photographing.*

Editor: Paul Mason
Designer: David Armitage

First published in 1990 by
Wayland (Publishers) Limited
61 Western Road, Hove
East Sussex BN3 IJD, England

British Library Cataloguing in Publication Data
Wolmar, Christian
    Censorship. – (Points of view)
    I. Censorship
    I. Title II. Series
    363.31

ISBN 0 7502 0003 0

Phototypeset by Direct Image Photosetting Ltd,
Hove, East Sussex, England
Printed in Italy by G. Canale & C.S.p.A., Turin
Bound in France by A.G.M.

Many people think that the views of racists, such as these Ku Klux Klan members, should be censored.

In fact, the concept of censorship raises a lot of complex issues. It is easy to say that all censorship is bad and the right to say or print anything should always be upheld. But there is a consensus in society that some displays of violence and sex, publication of personal attacks, some information about government policies and so on should be withheld from the general public. There is also agreement that laws which prevent people from inciting violence through racist publications or speeches are a good thing. The question is where the line should be drawn and by whom.

The problem of censorship becomes one of striking a balance between competing rights and, possibly, duties. There will always be debate and disagreement about where the balance is to be struck.

The right to freedom of expression is upheld by Article 19 of the Universal Declaration of Human Rights. This says:

> Everyone has the right to freedom of opinion and expression; this right includes freedom to hold opinions without interference and to seek, receive and impart information and ideas through any media and regardless of frontiers.

The Declaration was first adopted in 1948 but censorship has existed for much longer. The word itself comes from 'censor', the title of an official in Ancient Rome whose duty was to supervise public morals. According to the Oxford English Dictionary, one of the definitions of a censor is:

> . . . an official whose duty it is to inspect books, journals, plays, etc. before publication to secure that they shall contain nothing immoral, heretical or offensive or injurious to the state.

The Christian religion is not always peace loving. For centuries those whose views were unorthodox risked being burned at the stake, as this film clip shows.

Of course, before the days of the printing press, let alone the invention of radio and TV, there was precious little to censor. After the invention of the printing press by Gutenberg in the mid-fifteenth century, information became easier to disseminate. The Church, which played a central part in the life of the people, began to act as a censor, as it had done in the later days of the Roman Empire:

> Once established as the official religion of Rome, the Church itself made haste to consolidate its position by suppressing all competing views and dissent, which it labelled 'heresy'. This meant, among other things, strict control over the dissemination and interpretation of the Holy Scriptures which entailed censorship. (Michael Scammell, 'Censorship and its History, a Personal View', Article 19, *World Report 1988*.)

Within forty years of the invention of the printing press, the Church's first list or index of banned books was issued by the Inquisition, a religious court which existed for 600 years from 1232 until the early nineteenth century. The Inquisition imposed very strict censorship over what views could be held and the penalty for disobeying them was often death at the stake after hideous torture.

Arguments over religious views are still very much a feature of modern day life, as illustrated by the fuss over Salman Rushdie's book *The Satanic Verses* (see the chapter on religion). Indeed, the index of banned books which was first made binding on Roman Catholics in 1559 still exists today, in an altered form.

Torquemada
Torquemada, who died in 1498, was the most infamous of the Spanish inquisitors. Between 1483 and 1498, while Torquemada was in command, 8,800 were burned at the stake and 96,504 suffered less severe penalties. Some historians put the number of people burned at 10,000.

Censors are not just people with big black pens cutting out information they don't like from books or letters or with scissors chopping out bits of film or video. As well as government officials, they can be the owners of publications, judges, editors, advertisers or even the writers themselves. Nor are they always in far-off foreign countries ruled by dictatorships. Here are some examples from Britain:

> In 1935, a pacifist film was banned in 'the interests of public order'.

In 1935, Sotheby's were unable to auction original letters of Lord Nelson to the Duke of Wellington on the grounds that they were 'official secrets'.

In 1958, two Oxford graduates were sent to prison for detailing their experiences of National Service.

In 1965, the film 'Fanny Hill' was refused a certificate by the Board of Censors.

In 1980, a new edition Ordnance Survey map shows that a bomb factory at Burghfield near Reading shown on previous editions of the map has been replaced by two streams flowing into the Thames. (Amnesty International, British Section Education Project, *Censorship.*)

This book looks at the different motives for restricting the right to total free expression, such as political ideology; religious objections; concern over obscenity; libel and the requirements of wartime. It also examines the different ways censorship operates in the various media - TV, videos, film and newspapers.

1 *You are the editor of the school magazine and you have been given documents showing that the school's exam results are very bad. Why might it be a good idea to publish them?*

2 *Can you justify laws which ban the publication of racist views? Should these be an exception to the right to freedom of speech?*

In the USA, despite freedom of speech being guaranteed by the Constitution, some political views have been censored.

Political censorship

One of the most common forms of censorship across the world is the suppression of political views which are contrary to those of the government in power. With the secret police, the army, and the whole power of government behind them, repressive regimes can ensure that few views different from their own ever see the light of day. Thousands of journalists, writers and editors have died at the hands of death squads, the police and the army in countries across the world.

The country which had devised the most repressive tactics in modern times to prevent the expression of views was Romania, under the Ceausescu regime. This was overthrown during Christmas 1989. The state had placed incredible controls on the use and ownership of the basic tools of mass communication, such as photocopiers, typewriters and even typewriter ribbons:

> A decree of 1983 which empowers the Romanian authorities to decide who may or may not possess a typewriter is the most restrictive of its kind known [in the world]. The Ministry of Internal Affairs, through the local militia, maintains records on the production, use and maintenance of duplicators, typewriters, ink, typewriter ribbons and other materials for the reproduction of printed matter.

Romania placed very strict controls on freedom of speech. In December 1989 the people of Romania overthrew the government in a popular revolution.

In South Africa non-whites are daily denied human rights.

Individuals may, once they have permission, own a typewriter but to buy one he or she must apply to the local militia. The right to own a typewriter can be refused on the grounds that the individual has a police record, or that his or her behaviour poses a threat to public order or state security. (Kevin Boyle, *World Report 1988*.)

South Africa still has ways of keeping its citizens quiet. Its policy of apartheid not only keeps the races apart, ensuring the minority white population has the best of everything - from beaches and buses to schools and colleges - but under a law passed in 1950, the government has wide-ranging powers to 'ban' people who express views opposed to apartheid:

> Once a banning order is served, the victim cannot be quoted in any way, whether in newspapers, books or on radio and television. He or she is not allowed to prepare any statement for publication. A variety of other restrictions go with banning from prohibitions on attending meetings, entering schools, universities and factories to being ordered to remain at home within set hours. (*World Report*.)

Censorship in South Africa

The *New Nation* is a fortnightly newspaper established by a group of black people in South Africa in 1986. Within weeks of its launch, the South African authorities arrested and detained the editor, Zwelakhe Sisulu, for three weeks. He was released but later rearrested and held indefinitely. The explanation from the police was that 'he wrote articles which were designed to create an atmosphere conducive to unrest'. The newspaper was an instant success, building up to a circulation of 60,000 by the end of its first year. In March 1988, the government suspended publication of the *New Nation* for three months for allegedly promoting revolution. Sisulu was released in December 1988 but was not allowed to work as a journalist.

The South African government restricts information in many ways. Here a policeman is preventing a video being made of a demonstration.

9

While in Western countries such as the UK and the USA there are not such obvious and widespread restrictions on the right to freedom of expression, censorship still exists in various forms. The UK, unlike the USA, has no legal requirement for freedom of information. In the UK, government information is generally kept secret unless there is a good reason why it should be available, while in the USA information is generally available unless there is a good reason why it should be secret.

The lack of a constitutional right to freedom of expression in the UK was highlighted by two events there in the 1980s: the banning of the book *Spycatcher* and the ban on broadcasting the voices of members of Sinn Fein, the political wing of the Irish Republican Army (IRA).

Spycatcher was written by a former member of the secret service, Peter Wright. It outlined a series of incredible actions carried out by spies working for the UK government such as phone tapping, bugging and propaganda wars against the USSR and some of the UK's allies, for example France. It even detailed preparations for a coup attempt against Harold Wilson, the Labour Party prime minister, in the mid-1970s.

Peter Wright, his wife and his lawyer going to court in Australia. The UK government tried to stop his book, Spycatcher, *being published.*

The book that is banned in Britain!

Viking

The UK government justified its attempts to ban *Spycatcher* through a series of court actions by claiming that Wright was bound to secrecy:

> Civil servants are under an obligation to keep the confidences which they [obtain] in the course of their official duties; not only the maintenance of trust between ministers and civil servants but also the efficiency of government depend on their doing so. (Advice to civil servants in 1985 from Sir Robert Armstrong, then head of the Civil Service.)

The affair became increasingly ridiculous as large numbers of copies of the book published in Ireland and the USA flooded into the UK. Those opposed to the ban were adamant that it should be published there because it revealed a number of misdoings by the state and the secret services:

> Wright and his henchmen destroyed a number of careers; their secret inquisitions drove one Labour MP to suicide and another minister out of the Wilson Government. [But] the judges [in the trial] contented themselves with reviling Wright for treachery. (Geoffrey Robertson, *Freedom, the Individual and the Law,* 1989.)

While the UK government was trying to make sure people in the UK were unable to read Spycatcher, *it was on sale in many other countries.*

Angered by continuous terrorist attacks by the IRA in Northern Ireland, the British government decided in 1988 to ban spokespeople of Sinn Fein from appearing on radio or television. However, although their voices cannot be transmitted, it is possible for the news organizations to dub reports of what they say with actors' voices. The ban has been widely criticized because Sinn Fein attracts significant numbers of votes in both local and national elections in Northern Ireland:

> Sinn Fein is a political fact of life in Northern Ireland . . . The ban deprives viewers and listeners of the contribution radio and television can make to a full understanding of their political landscape. The ban must make audiences wary of a broadcasting service that does not have the independence to reflect reality as they know it . . . By comparison with the scale of restriction that operates in the USSR and South Africa, the Sinn Fein ban is but a small step; but it crosses a line that governments in democratic societies should not cross. (John Birt, deputy director general of the BBC, the *Daily Telegraph*, 16 October 1989.)

The US Freedom of Information Act, which was passed in 1966 and strengthened in 1974, forces government officials to say why information should not be released. There is a growing list of exemptions but nevertheless the law has attracted the criticism of officials who think it lets out secrets that could affect national security. Defenders of the Act say that its benefits greatly outweigh its disadvantages:

The UK government also tried, successfully, to ban the direct quotation of members of the IRA. Republicans in Northern Ireland were forced to use other methods of mass communication, such as this wall mural.

The ban on quoting members of the IRA has caused a great deal of anger in Northern Ireland, as this demonstration shows.

> For all the talk that Freedom of Information Act disclosures have disrupted criminal investigations, encouraged industrial espionage or even allowed a foreign power to obtain national security secrets, the Act's critics have offered few, if any, examples of government documents that were released with harmful results under the Act. On the other hand, there are numerous examples of stories the American people would never have learned about their own government if journalists, public interest organizations and individual citizens could not use the Freedom of Information Act to obtain government documents. (David Kusnet and Steve Katz, *Champaign-Urbana News Gazette,* 8 October 1986.)

In the USA, there is also a constitutional freedom to express views. A Supreme Court ruling said:

> If there is any fixed star in our constitutional constellation, it is that no official, high or petty, can prescribe what shall be orthodox in politics, nationalism, religion or other matters of opinion or force citizens to confess by word or act their faith therein.

This principle is expressed in the First Amendment to the Constitution:

> Congress shall make no law respecting an establishment of religion, or prohibiting the free exercise thereof; or abridging the freedom of speech or of the press; or the right of the people peaceably to assemble and to petition the government for a redress of grievances.

But it has not always been upheld, and as the chapter on war shows, laws passed to maintain national security during wartime have remained in force long after the war is finished.

1 **What are the possible arguments for and against the Sinn Fein ban and the publication of Spycatcher?**

2 **How does a Freedom of Information Act make a journalist's job easier? Do you think it can be abused?**

3 **How can repressive governments stop journalists from writing what they want?**

The power of the owners

It is not only governments that place restraints on the freedom of the press. In the UK and the USA, ownership of newspapers is concentrated in the hands of a few multinational companies headed by media moguls like Rupert Murdoch and Robert Maxwell. They ensure that it is their own political views which dominate the coverage:

> Of the eleven national [UK] dailies, seven are owned by four companies. Of the nine national Sundays, four are owned by two companies . . . While it is true that writers and commentators of the left find space in the papers of the right, and it is also true that much reporting in the broadsheet papers is accurate and full, the dominant tone is right of centre. (John Lloyd, *Index on Censorship*.)

   This concentration of ownership and views makes it difficult for journalists and writers to make their voices heard if they have strong political views contrary to those of the owner.

Above *Robert Maxwell, media mogul.* **Below** *The* Observer's *response when its owner was not allowed to buy Harrods of London.*

The lone stand taken by The Observer

THE OBSERVER, SUNDAY 15 JUNE 1986

BUSINESS

33

The history of the Egyptian Al-Fayed family, owners of Harrods, is traced back through the shifting desert sands

In search of the fabulous Pharaohs

PETER WICKMAN, a former correspondent for *Stern*, was assigned to Egypt in search of the Fayed dynasty. He...

The bloody Harrods battle

THE OUTCOME of the bloodiest corporate war ever waged in the United King...

Amid allegations and acrimony, the 7-year Harrods war reaches its climax. ...KUS reports

The Observer defeats Al-Fayed injunction

by LORANA SULLIVAN

JUSTICE MANN ruled on ...day that *The Observer* should not ...topped from publishing further ...les in connection with the ...spaper's consistent ...the Egyptian ...not fi...

Fayeds called to account on loans

by MELVYN MARCKUS, City Editor, and LORANA SULLIVAN

DESPITE the vast reputed wealth of Egyptian businessman Mohamed Al-Fayed and his two brothers, records filed at Companies House reveal that House... cent stake in House of Fraser to the Al-Fayeds after its own attempts to acquire House of Fraser were frustrated by the Government. *The Observer*, which is owned by Lon... ...has received two libel writs ...Al-Fay...

overdraft of £900,000 ...purchase c. 34.4 million

loans from Mohamed, Salah and Ali Al-Fayed and by bank borrowings.' Rowland has constantly challenged the content of Kleinwort's offer document, dated 23 March 1985. In a recent letter dated 21 April 1986 to Michael Hawkes, chairman of Kleinwort Benson, Rowland all...

total outstanding bank loans were refinanced through a term-loan and guarantee facility of £... million, part of which is secured on the assets of the company,' a footnote states. 'This facility expires on 30 June 1988 and interest is payable on amounts drawn at rates varying with the London Inter-Bank Offered ...In order to reflect overseas

In the UK, owners of newspapers have frequently been accused of using them for their own commercial ends. For example, the *Observer,* a left-of-centre Sunday newspaper owned by the huge Lonrho company, has given extensive coverage to a story about Harrods, the London department store. Lonrho's chief executive, 'Tiny' Rowland, had been stopped by the government from buying Harrods. In the USA, newspapers and local TV stations are increasingly owned by large corporations which have been accused of using access to the mass media to serve their own interests:

> A typical medium circulation newspaper makes a 23 per cent profit each year. The American press can hardly pretend to be a critic of giant US corporations and exorbitant business profits, since the press enjoys profits that equal those of most oil companies. (Michael Parenti, 'Does the US have a Free Press?' *The Witness,* 1985.)

Book publishers have also been accused of influencing the views that end up in print:

> Of course there is no official government stamp on what is written or printed in the USA. American authors are not subject to Soviet-style psychological pressure to conform or exiled because of what they attempt to publish. Instead . . . American authors encounter economic pressures that can seriously affect the contents of their writing. (Herbert Mitgang, *Dangerous Dossiers,* 1989.)

Media ownership in the USA

In the USA, 10 huge business and financial corporations control the 3 major television and radio networks, 34 subsidiary television stations, 201 cable television systems, 62 radio stations, 20 record companies, 59 magazines including *Time* and *Newsweek,* 58 newspapers including the *Washington Post* and the *New York Times,* 41 book publishers and various motion picture companies like Columbia Pictures and Twentieth Century Fox.

The frustration of sacked workers often leads to clashes with the police.

The result, according to many commentators, is that there is little room for political debate in the US media:

> Compared to the vibrant and diverse political perspectives available in European news, their American counterparts are embarrassingly homogeneous. Political variations in the three US networks' broadcasts may only be detectable in measurements of parts per billion. Each sits astride the same political fence, frightened to lean to either side in order not to offend views - or more importantly, not to offend sponsors. Peter Dykstra, *Greenpeace,* 1987.)

Nevertheless, there are some who defend the increasing concentration of ownership, saying that it makes the industry more efficient and does not make the press less free:

> It is true that many important stories are not published and some of them would be poor publicity for big business. But there is no hard evidence that the choices that must be made to cope with an oversupply of news are dictated by narrow self-interest. In fact, many recent broadcasts, movies, magazines and newspaper features have carried stories critical of business. Similarly the charge that business interests are responsible for the general support by media personnel of the existing political system is not borne out. It seems much more likely that American journalists in large organizations, like their colleagues in small, independently-owned enterprises are interested in appealing to their audience and so reflect the values of mainstream American society. (Doris Graber, 'Mass Media and American Politics', *Congressional Quarterly,* 1984.)

1 Doris Graber (above) says that American journalists 'reflect the values of mainstream American society.' Do you think these are the only values that should be reflected in the media?

2 Have you ever censored something you have written or said, in case it might offend someone or get you in trouble? If you were a journalist, would you be prepared to censor yourself in order to avoid offending your employer? Why do owners try to censor what their employees say?

4

Censorship and war

> It is commonly accepted that governments can legitimately withhold information on the grounds that its release might endanger nationals' lives. The grey area, however, is in defining the scope of the categories. (David Morrison and Howard Tumler, *Journalists at War*, 1988.)

Wartime is presented as a special case. The fight against a common enemy forces people to accept stricter censorship than during peacetime. The reason is that any government at war wants to prevent the publication or spread of information which might be useful to its enemy. But the choice of what should be allowed and what banned is a very difficult one. Withholding too much information can allow government policies or military mistakes to be covered up. One of the earliest and most famous war correspondents, William Howard Russell of *The Times*, alerted the British public to the disastrous state of the Crimean War campaign:

> William Howard Russell dared to tell the English-speaking peoples that our little army was perishing from want of proper food and clothing. He probably made mistakes as his statements were hurriedly written. He incurred much enmity but few unprejudiced men [would now deny that] by awakening the conscience of the British nation, he saved the remnant of those great battalions. (Sir Edward Cook, *The Press in Wartime*, 1920.)

When the General Belgrano was sunk off the coast of Argentina the UK government refused to release much information. It has since been claimed that the ship was not heading towards the war zone as the government suggested, but away from it.

At the time of the US invasion of Grenada little information and few pictures were released.

In the American Civil War, the country was divided, with supporters of the North living in the South and vice versa, and censorship was widely practised. Newspapers were simply banned from publishing articles which criticized their own side.

That was before the days of army censors sitting over journalists to make sure that no military secrets were revealed. In the First World War, all communications from journalists at the front had to go through an army censor. And a censorship board which had three departments - dealing with cable, postal and press communications - was set up. Not only were newspapers censored, they were not even allowed to refer to the fact that articles had been removed or changed.

Of more recent wars, Vietnam and the Falklands, or Malvinas, offer contrasting experiences. The USA's war in Vietnam lasted from 1963 to 1975 and was given saturation coverage on television. It is felt by many people that the uncensored reports coming from the battlefront so influenced public opinion that they forced the USA to concede defeat and pull out of the war:

> Maybe the historians will agree that the reporters and the cameras were decisive in the end. They brought the issue of the war to the people, before the Congress or the courts, and forced the withdrawal of US power from Vietnam. (James Renton, *New York Times,* 30 April 1975.)

At first people in the USA accepted the war in Vietnam. Later on huge protests became commonplace.

This view of war coverage is not universal. Other people feel that gory pictures of the dead and the wounded in wars will strengthen popular support for it:

> There is no evidence to suggest that showing the horrors of war act as a brake on existing wars or indeed make wars in the future less likely. In fact, from historical evidence the counter-hypothesis that the graphic portrayal of destruction is more likely to stiffen resolve to fight and foster the revengeful desire to inflict further destruction is a stronger candidate for support. *(Journalists at War.)*

How do you think pictures like this one of a Vietnamese priest protesting about the war would make you feel?

These Cuban prisoners on Grenada only have a piece of plastic as shelter. At the time no one knew they were being treated in this way.

That was not the opinion of the UK government during its conflict with Argentina in the Falkland Islands, or Malvinas. No immediate TV pictures were allowed to be shown. Instead, film of the battles was transmitted weeks later and there were few shots of injured, let alone dead, UK troops. Information about setbacks such as the sinking of ships or the downing of aircraft was delayed for many hours, because of alleged fears that the information would help the Argentines. The lack of frankness of the government attracted criticism both at the time and after the event:

> Ian Macdonald [the government spokesman] said of the bombing of Stanley airfield on 1 May, in a raid by Vulcan B2 aircraft from Ascension and Harriers from the task force, 'British forces had taken action designed to enforce the total exclusion zone and deny the Argentines the use of the airstrip at Port Stanley.' It is hard to see what secrets would be given away by a more direct statement that the airfield had been bombed.' (Valerie Adams, *The Media and the Falklands Campaign,* 1986.)

Dead but not dead

During the last [second world] war, a committee used to meet every Friday night at Woburn Abbey and concoct between forty and fifty lies to be dispensed around the world the following week. On 26 September 1941, a batch of twelve was approved all suggesting that Germany's allies were deserting her. Number 445, for example, said: 'Twelve Romanian generals have been shot for giving their troops orders to return to Romania'. This lie was duly disseminated and on October 7, the *Evening News* ran the headline 'Twelve Romanian Generals Shot Dead.' (The *Independent Magazine,* 2 October 1989.)

Similarly, during the USA invasion of Grenada - a much quicker and less bloody affair - journalists were kept away from the scene of the battles until several days after the invasion.

There is a saying that the first casualty of war is the truth. Indeed, at times of war, not only is information strictly censored, but stories which may help 'the cause' are invented. (See box.)

For a very limited war far away from the homeland, like the Falklands/Malvinas, Grenada or Vietnam, life was not greatly different in the USA or the UK except for people directly involved. In both world wars, though, the news media were severely curtailed at home. Although few would disagree on the need for some censorship, it is hard to ensure that it is relaxed afterwards. The measures instituted in the First World War in the USA were used for the whole period up to the Second World War to suppress the expression of opinion and meetings by radicals and communists:

> The lasting threat to America's democratic government is in the carry over into peacetime of repressive measures instituted during war. When peacetime came, the repressive measures, instead of being abolished, were used by federal, state and municipal officials and imitated by social, political and municipal groups. These agencies employed censorship ideas and techniques against their domestic foes under the guise of protecting the institution of the US and the American way of life. (James R Mock, *Censorship 1917, 1941*.)

> 1 Why are the military authorities so concerned with secrecy during a time of war?
>
> 2 Make up a news story which you think would have been helpful to the Germans and Japanese during the Second World War.

Senator McCarthy of the USA. He used laws that were designed to stop Nazi propaganda in the Second World War, to persecute people whose political views were left wing.

5

Religion and blasphemy

Like sex and politics, religion inspires firmly held views. It is, therefore, a natural hunting ground for censors. In the USA, for example, it was long forbidden to teach Darwinism, the view that people are descended from monkeys, in schools. This was because it is in direct contradiction to the story told in the Bible, which says that on the sixth day God created people.

Indeed, the issue is still a live one. During the 1980s, a reading series was attacked by Christian fundamentalists in Tennessee who claimed that the requirement that their children read certain books violated their religious rights. The books included a wide range of literature. In Alabama, forty-four textbooks were banned from schools for the teaching of 'the religion of secular humanism.'

Fundamentalists in the USA complaining that their children are taught about evolution at school, which contradicts what the Bible says.

When Salman Rushdie's book The Satanic Verses was released, Muslims all around the world joined demonstrations against it. This one is in Iran, outside the UK Embassy.

In the UK blasphemy has been a crime since 1617, when John Taylor was put in the stocks for denouncing Christ as a whoremaster and orthodox religion as a cheat. The only prosecution in modern times was in 1979 and concerned a poem published in the newspaper *Gay News*. The poem, by Professor James Kirkup, used the imagery of physical love to convey his feeling of union with his God. The judge in the case, which resulted in a successful prosecution, defined blasphemy as any writing,

> . . . concerning God or Christ, the Christian religion, the Bible, or some sacred subject, using words which are scurrilous, abusive or offensive and which tend to vilify the Christian religion (and therefore have a tendency to lead to a breach of the peace).

The law was seen as 'unsatisfactory and archaic' by the British Law Commission, a body of legal experts which regularly reviews laws. The Commission recommended recently that blasphemy should be abolished. As early as 1949, one of Britain's foremost judges said:

> The reason for this law was because it was thought that a denial of Christianity was liable to shake the fabric of society, which was itself founded on Christian religion. There is no such danger to society now and the offence of blasphemy is a dead letter.' (Lord Denning.)

Blasphemy only applies to texts that insult the Christian religion, a fact that was highlighted by the Salman Rushdie affair. Rushdie's book, *The Satanic Verses,* was thought to be so offensive by some Muslims that they burnt it in public. The Ayatollah Khomeini, then the leader of Iran, imposed a death sentence on the author for having insulted Mohammed. The extreme anti-Rushdie view was summed up in this way by one prominent Muslim:

> What he has written is far worse to Muslims than if he'd raped one's own daughter. It's an assault on every Muslim's inner being . . . It's like a knife being dug into you or being raped yourself.' (Dr Zaki Badawi, chairman of the Islamic Law Council, the *Guardian,* 27 February 1989.)

Two leaders of the Muslim community in the UK protest outside Downing Street.

The Monty Python film The Life of Brian *was attacked as blasphemous by leaders of the Christian religion.*

The strong feelings aroused by the Rushdie book immediately led to calls for blasphemy to be extended to other religions. An English Member of Parliament, Tony Benn, pointed out the problems in making such an extension:

> The idea of extending the offence of blasphemy to cover all religions would require a tight legal definition of what is religion and could open up a nightmare of endless court cases which, if they succeeded, would silence all humanists, atheists, heretics and free-thinkers. (the *Guardian,* 7 April 1989.)

While there was a world-wide campaign in favour of Rushdie, some writers were not sure that he should have written the book because, as a former Muslim, Rushdie knew that it would insult Muslims:

> Clearly he has profound knowledge of the Muslim religion and its people and he must have been totally aware of the deep and violent feelings his book would stir up among Muslims. In other words, he knew exactly what he was doing and he cannot plead otherwise. This kind of sensationalism does indeed get an indifferent book on to the top of the best sellers list but to my mind it is a cheap way of doing it. It also puts a severe strain on the very proper principle that the writer has an absolute right to say what he likes. In a civilized world, we all have a moral obligation to apply a modicum of censorship to our own work in order to reinforce this principle of free speech. (Roald Dahl, letter to *The Times,* 28 February 1989.)

Life under strict religious censorship

Suppose you are living in Geneva, Switzerland in the year 1553. You can expect a minister and an elder to visit you and your family once a year and these men will question you about the most intimate details of your way of living. You may not frequent taverns or dance or sing "indecent or irreligious" songs. You are cautioned against excesses in entertainment, extravagance in living and immodesty in dress. The law even specifies how many different items can be served at one meal . . . Books which are considered wrong in religious tenets or tending toward immorality are not available to you. You may not attend any theatrical performances.' (Eli Oboler, *The Fear of the Word; Censorship and Sex,* 1974.)

The issues raised by the Rushdie case bring out the fundamental question of freedom of expression:

> If the assassins succeed in finding him and killing him, it will be a great defeat for thought and freedom. There are principles we cannot compromise. Freedom to imagine, to create and to write is one of them. If what he portrays injures and hurts personal beliefs or convictions, the public is not only free not to read the work, it is also free to sue the author for libel . . .
> Who can seriously believe that a religion as prestigious and alive as Islam, which has more than a billion believers throughout the world, could be threatened by a work of fiction? Can a novel, even if it is blasphemous, shake 1,500 years of history? (Tahar Ben Jelloun, Le Monde, 3 March 1989.)

1 Why do people who have strong religious views try to restrict other opinions?

2 What are the problems with extending the law of blasphemy to other religions? Are there problems with abolishing the law altogether?

Some people have questioned an author's right to write what he or she wants if it will stir up this much hatred. What do you think?

6

Obscenity

Obscenity is at the root of many, possibly the majority, of censorship debates. But what is obscenity? We all have our own ideas about it:

> We live in an age where one person's obscenity is another person's bedtime video. The deep division in society over the appropriate limit to . . . permissiveness is mirrored by an inconsistent and largely ineffectual censorship of material which may offend or entertain, corrupt or enlighten, according to the taste and character of individual readers and viewers. *(Freedom, the Individual and the Law.)*

Although most commonly used to describe displays of sexual explicitness, obscenity is not only about sex. Obscenity is, according to the dictionary, anything which is 'indecent . . . tending to deprave or corrupt' and is often used to describe violent images, especially on film and TV, where it is particularly easy to show very violent scenes. These themes will be discussed in greater depth in chapter seven.

There are sex shops such as this one in most cities. Many people find them offensive and claim that they are harmful to society.

Because of this problem over the nature of obscenity the US Supreme Court has never even tried to define it.

> Obscenity is at once the most familiar and the most elusive concept in law and social life. On the one hand, it's widely supposed that nearly everyone has a notion of obscenity and would consider certain utterances or materials to be proscribable. On the other hand, the concept has an ambiguity that prevents the sort of precise formulation that is desirable in framing a reference for meting out criminal penalties and for limiting freedom of speech. *(Censorship in the Movies*, Richard S Randall.)

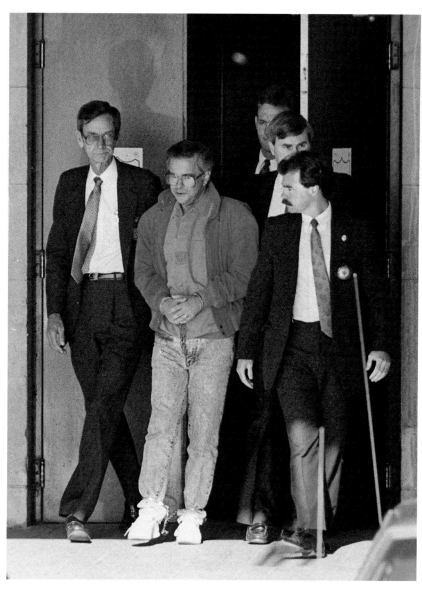

Jim Bakker, the US fundamentalist preacher, leaving court on his way to prison for tax evasion. Fundamentalists often claim to hold the moral high ground. Should they tell others how to act?

In Britain, in the thirty years after the Second World War, there was a series of famous prosecutions over the concept of obscenity, which brought into question the writings of great authors such as James Joyce and DH Lawrence. The prosecutions were generally unsuccessful and, like the legal cases over *Spycatcher* (see chapter two), attracted vast amounts of publicity for the books concerned:

> The censorship of art and literature in Britain until the 1960s at least had the one great merit of bringing James Joyce and Henry Miller and DH Lawrence to the excited attention of generations of schoolchildren. *(Freedom, the Individual and the Law.)*

Those prosecutions were attempts by religious and other conservative groups to stop what they saw as obscene material falling into the hands of young people. These prosecutions of what many people see as great literature are unlikely to be repeated in the West during these more open and liberated times, but there is still a very strong body of opinion against allowing sexually explicit material to be available:

> There are a number of entirely reasonable claims that can be made in favour of some degree of public reticence about sexual matters . . . The colourful display of erotic magazines at local shops and news-stands is offensive to many. Would there be any loss of liberty to require them to be encased in Cellophane, and placed on racks above the reach of children or be confined for sale to licensed sex shops? This is the kind of administrative control that operates in many countries. *(Freedom, the Individual and the Law.)*

This statue is on public display in Italy. Some people would call images of naked men pornography. Do you consider this pornography or art?

Strip bars such as this are common. Do you think they affect the way women are seen by society?

Clare Short, MP, whose attempt to outlaw pictures of naked women in newspapers failed. There are very few women in the UK Parliament. Do you think this affected the outcome of the vote?

Those seeking restrictions on the availability of pornography have two main motives - they fear that its availability encourages sexual crimes such as rape and they are concerned that the depiction of women in this way is oppressive and insulting to women:

> All pornography says [to men] women ask for it, they enjoy it, they are not equal to you, they are objects you throw away. This affects women's perceptions of themselves and their ability to achieve a sense of worth. (Sam Chugg quoted in the *Guardian*, 15 February 1990.)

But some people argue that there is little evidence to support a direct link between pornography and crime:

> The rising trend in sexual offences generally, including rape and sexual assaults, started long before pornography began to be widely available. The increase in sexual offences has been significantly slower in the last twenty years than in crime generally. (Excerpt from research commissioned for UK government.)

It is clear there is a strong feeling among most women that pornography oppresses them and is likely to encourage men to treat them as less than equal. British newspapers like the *Sun* which portray pictures of topless women - known as page three girls because that is the page they normally appear on - have come under fire. A Member of Parliament, Clare Short, tried to bring in a new law which would have stopped 'the display of pictures of naked or partially naked women in sexually provocative poses.'

Woman magazine conducted a survey and found an overwhelming majority of women supported the ban:

> Four out of five respondents to the *Woman* survey believed there was a link between page three pictures and violence against women. There is a gut certainty that the image the pictures represented of women - passive, available, just there for sex - increase men's view of women as 'game' - for sex and violence. (Melissa Benn, 'Page Three and the Campaign against it', in Gail Chester and Julienne Dickey, *Feminism and Censorship*, 1988.)

In defence of the pictures, Samantha Fox, a famous topless model, said they were:

> quite harmless. Page three girls aren't doing anything in the pictures that they aren't doing on the beach. They're clean, happy pictures . . . It's always what you hide that people are after. It used to be ankles. In fact, maybe kids will think about nudity in a nice way because of them. (*Woman* 24 May 1986).

Displays of homosexuality or even literature about homosexuality have long been a concern of educators and politicians. In Britain, Section 28 of a new Local Government Act was passed in 1988. It aimed to prevent homosexuality from being presented in a positive way in schools. The Act said that teachers should not 'intentionally promote homosexuality or publish material with the intention of promotion of homosexuality.'

Sam Fox, a topless model who has made enough money to buy a London wine bar and launch a singing career.

A demonstration against Section 28 of the Local Government Act, which outlaws the 'promotion of homosexuality'.

The result has been that plays have been banned and organizations helping gay men and lesbians have lost their funding. Here is one example of censorship which has resulted from the Act:

> On September 23, 1988, a production of 'Trapped in Time', due to be performed by the Avon Touring Theatre Company in a secondary school, was cancelled by the school's head teacher. The play, which examines the way different people have been represented in history . . . includes a short scene called 'Queen Victoria's coming out' in which one of the characters tells his friends that he is gay. In banning the play, the head teacher expressed concern that he might be in breach of Section 28 if he allowed the performance to go ahead. (Madeleine Colvin, 'Section 28', in *Liberty,* the National Council for Civil Liberties.)

1 Suggest arguments for and against the inclusion of photographs of topless women in newspapers. Do you think such newspapers should be kept out of the reach of children in shops and wrapped in Cellophane?

2 Why do you think there are no suggestive pictures of men on page five of newspapers that feature page three girls?

3 Who do you think should decide what teenagers can see and read: the government, teachers, parents or teenagers themselves?

A demonstration in Berlin, protesting about the denial of rights to homosexual men and women. When homosexuals start to talk about their sexuality, their views are often suppressed.

Film and TV censorship

Films attracted the attention of the censors from their earliest days because of their powerful impact. In the USA between 1934 and 1968 films were rigidly controlled by a body called the Production Code Administration, more commonly known as the Hays Office, after Will Hays, the man who ran it. Set up by the film industry itself because of fears that otherwise the government would bring in stricter censorship laws, it imposed serious restrictions on what could be shown. Story lines had to follow certain patterns - for example, criminals always had to be caught, kidnapped children always had to be returned unharmed and suicide was to be discouraged. Many plots of Shakespeare plays would have failed the tests imposed by the Production Code. Controls at times appeared to lack any logic:

> The Hollywood censors, with the arrogance of a monarchal decree, had arbitrarily set thirty seconds as the maximum length of a screen kiss. When the stopwatch touched thirty, you passed from the romantic to the obscene. (Gerald Gardner, *The Censorship Papers.*)

Future US President Reagan sleeping in a separate bed in order to conform to the Hays code, while Diana Lynn sleeps with the chimp. The clip is from Bedtime for Bonzo.

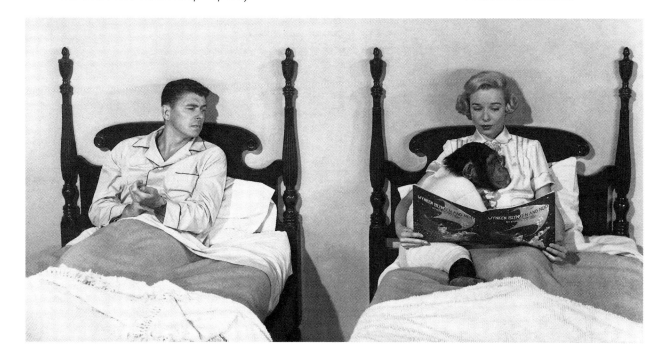

The orgy scene from the Cecil B de Mille film The Ten Commandments. *De Mille used biblical stories to get round the censors.*

Film makers used all sorts of devices to get round the censorship rules and used to play games with the censors:

> With the exception of Busby Berkeley, who end-ran [outwitted] the censors by relying on leggy chorus girls, the most successful evader of the Hays Office was Cecil B De Mille. He did this through the inspired expedient of telling biblical stories. The most pious audience of censors, women's clubs, congressmen, clergymen or editorial writers were disarmed by sin and sensation, if [the plot was taken from] the Good Book. Normally a scene of orgy, rape, depravity and perversion would send the reformers out shouting for scalps; but when the tale was ostensibly lifted from the Bible, the censors said 'Amen'. *(The Censorship Papers.)*

In 1968, the censorship rules in the USA were relaxed and a system of classification similar to the UK one was introduced. Although the classification letters are similar, the two systems are in practice quite different. For example, sometimes a film which is given a PG (parental guidance) classification in the USA will get a stricter '18' one in the UK or vice versa. The USA censors are more worried about sex, while the UK Board of Film Classification is more concerned with violence.

Here is a passage from the Board's 1988 annual report which explains its thinking when making cuts in films.

> Few psychologists now suggest that screen violence has a direct cause and effect relationship with the sort of real violence which may endanger society. Instead, the media are seen as one of many influences in the complex equation that leads to violence in the streets or the home. The problem for media regulators is to weigh up the rights of film makers to convey their messages with all the freedom society can offer against the risk that freedom to promote anti-social values may result in a significant loss of liberty for the victims of violence. Whose freedom takes priority in a free society, that of the communicator of violence or of the victim of those too easily influenced by violent messages?

Some examples of programmes which have been cut or banned from the BBC:
1980. Anti-nuclear campaigner EP Thompson has his invitation to deliver the Dimbleby Lecture on BBC television vetoed by the Director-General of the BBC.
1980. BBC decides not to transmit an Open University lecture, 'Towards the final abyss - a scientist's view of the arms race,' judging it 'inappropriate and unsuitable.'
1983. A BBC play, 'The Falklands Factor', has two minutes taken out before screening because the BBC says the section might have caused distress to the families of Falklands soldiers.
1987. BBC governors agree to drop a play about the Falklands because it is reported to be sympathetic to Mrs Thatcher and the BBC feels it impossible to broadcast it with a general election imminent.
(Index on Censorship.)

How do you think young children are affected by scenes such as this one from the film Predator?

In the UK the classification system was extended to videos because of pressure by religious and conservative groups anxious about the effect of violence and sex in videos on children. A report by a group of social scientists received very wide coverage which helped bring about the new law:

> A third of all seven year olds have watched the very nastiest of video horror films, according to a survey just published. Half of all fifteen year olds have seen at least one of these videos, which would never have been granted a certificate in a cinema. (*The Sunday Times*, 20 October 1985.)

That survey received such wide coverage that it resulted in the passing of the Video Recordings Act in 1985.

Few people would support the idea that children should be able to watch pornographic or violent films without restriction. Their effect is widely believed to be harmful. The researchers mentioned above found:

> Many children say they suffer from bad dreams the night after watching a horror film. Many more speak vividly of nightmares and often of the after-effects continuing for several days after having seen a particularly horrific film. (*Video Violence and Children*, report of a parliamentary group video inquiry.)

Do children really watch violent videos?
One of the researchers who worked on the survey (see p.36) rejected its findings. He said that the high figure for children supposedly watching these videos had been obtained by asking them about specific videos and cross-checked the information, by giving children another list of videos, some of which did not exist. He found that a high proportion said they had seen these non-existent films. The children had claimed to have watched the videos either out of ignorance or because they wanted to appear brave in front of their friends.

Freddy, the character who terrorizes sleeping children in their dreams in the Nightmare on Elm Street *films. Strangely, he has become a cult figure among children.*

Films censored in the UK
During 1988, the UK Board of Film Classification gave certificates to 337 feature films. Of these, 49 had to be cut in order to receive a certificate. Over 20 needed cuts in violence, 6 were cut because of real violence to animals which is illegal under UK law, and 10 were cut for their sexual content. During the same year, the Board gave certificates to 2,561 feature videos and refused one to 5.

Left *Do you think that seeing violent behaviour on television encourages real violence among children?*

The researchers also suggested:

> that children are adversely affected by their exposure to scenes of violence on video films; the viewing of scenes of extreme violence has an obsessive characteristic that may be habit forming; and that the evidence strongly suggests a causal link between the viewing of violence and violent behaviour. *(Video Violence and Children.)*

However, the link between watching violence and actually committing violent acts is difficult to prove.

> Studies have shown that aggressive adolescent boys are keener on violent programmes than non-aggressive boys. So do boys become violent because they watch violent television? Or do violent boys watch violent television because they enjoy it?' (Joan Smith, 'Mrs Mary Whitehouse's Private Member', the *New Statesman.)*

The censorship and control mechanisms for TV in the UK have been developed with twin aims in mind - to keep unsuitable material portraying sex and violence off the screens, particularly before 9 pm when young children may still be watching, and to keep a balance so that one political view is not given more favourable coverage.

1 *Should controls of what is shown on television, including videos, be stricter than controls on films?*

2 *What feelings do you have when you see people being violent on TV. Do they make you more or less likely to commit acts of violence?*

3 *Whose freedom do you think takes priority in a free society — that of the communicator of violence or that of the victim of those too easily influenced by violent messages?*

8

Libel and the right to reply

The libel, or defamation, laws are a major restriction on freedom of speech. But their purpose is to prevent people writing or saying untrue things about other individuals or organizations and they have been created to protect people from unfair attacks in the press.

There are two problems with the libel laws. One is that they tend to benefit only those rich and powerful enough to defend their reputation in court:

> In an important decision, the European Court of Human Rights endorsed the distinction between private personality and a public figure: politicians and celebrities ought to tolerate stronger comments on their activities than ordinary members of the public. However this distinction (accepted in the USA) is not widely recognized. Indeed, the reverse is the case. People holding high office, such as presidents, monarchs, heads of state, the military, and judges are protected by laws that make it a criminal offence, and occasionally an offence meriting the death penalty, to voice criticism. In many countries, defamation laws are a major constraint on reporting by the media. (*World Report.*)

The second problem with the libel laws is that fear of a libel action or prosecution can prevent many stories seeing the light of day either because, although true, they cannot be proved in court or because the subject of the story is known to sue for libel. There is a growing campaign for a reform of the libel laws on both sides of the Atlantic:

> Neither side wins much from the way libel works today. The law effectively chills both the press and private citizens who wish to speak out on public issues. It does this by imperiling those who cannot afford the risk of the possibility of huge court judgements or the certainty of ever-increasing defense fees . . . The sole purpose of libel law is the restoration of unjustly lost reputation . . . Among the changes I propose in this article are steps to encourage publishers to print corrections, limits on damages to amounts actually lost by those who sue and the adoption of a rule providing that the loser in libel cases should generally bear the costs of the case.

Tessa Sanderson, the Olympic javelin champion, who won a libel case over allegations that she had 'stolen' another woman's husband.

What is libel?
To libel somebody is to issue a statement in writing criticizing a person, or indeed a company, which is either untrue or cannot be proved in court and lowers their reputation. Although there is an offence of 'criminal libel', this is very rarely used, and most libels are resolved in the civil courts where the plaintiff - the person or company who has been criticized - takes the author, the publisher and perhaps even the printer and the distributor to court to seek damages.

With changes such as these we can avoid inhibiting speech while permitting those who should sue to do so. (Floyd Abrams, 'Why we should change the Libel Law', the *New York Times Magazine*, 1985.)

Robert Maxwell is rich enough to take people he feels have libelled him to court. What can those who are not so rich do?

In the UK, there is a Press Council, a body set up by newspapers to which people can complain. The Council has no powers to fine or discipline journalists, except to make the newspaper concerned publish its judgement. Because the Press Council has proved so weak, there have been moves to bring in a law which would give people the right to reply to articles which attack them.

The right of reply already exists in several countries:

> In France, the right of reply for both private citizens and representatives of organizations has been enshrined in law since 1881. Editors are required to 'insert within three days of receipt' the replies of any persons referred to in a daily newspaper or periodical, on pain of a fine. In West Germany, any person affected by a factual statement in a printed work can send the editor a signed statement of reply within three months. The reply must appear in the same section and typeface as the original offending text and will be printed as a letter to the editor. (Norman Buchan and Tricia Sumner, *Glasnost in Britain*, 1989.)

However, some campaigning journalists oppose the right of reply because they feel that, like the libel laws, it will be used against them more often than it will help them.

Elton John, who was awarded a million pounds in a recent libel case over allegations that he was cruel to his pets. Do you think this is a reasonable amount of money?

FURY AT RIPPER WIFE'S £600,000

Huge Private Eye payout

Blanket coverage . . . Sonia Sutcliffe yesterday after winning her case

Sam's assets insured for £¼m

IF YOU LOST AN EYE...

Ripper's wife . . . Sonia

By SHAN LANCASTER

YORKSHIRE Ripper's wife Sonia Sutcliffe won £600,000 libel damages yesterday — sparking fury at the staggering size of the payout.

£66,000 LOTTO: Numbers- Page 9 ● £31,000 BINGO: Numbers- Page 20

LIBEL SENSATION

THE Sun

Tuesday, May 15, 1984   16p   TODAY'S TV: PAGE 12

Members of all The Sun production chapels refused to handle the Arthur Scargill picture and major headline on our lead story. The Sun has decided, reluctantly, to print the paper without either.

By CHARLES RAE and BRIAN DIXON

£40,000 BINGO! Today's lucky numbers on Page 16

> I am against the right of reply. From my experience of regulatory bodies which exist outside the trade union movement, the Press Council is the best example, it seems to be quite clear that such bodies are used in the main by the powerful against those few occasions in the press where the powerful have been rumbled . . . (Paul Foot in *Glasnost in Britain.*)

In the days when the print trade unions were more powerful, they would often take the law into their own hands by refusing to work on articles which they found offensive or with which they disagreed. For example, during the 1984-5 miners' strike, the *Sun* wanted a picture of the miners' leader Arthur Scargill on the front page. He had one arm raised in what looked like a Nazi salute and the *Sun* used the headline 'Mine Führer', implying that he was a fascist by giving him the same title as Adolf Hitler had taken for himself. In fact, Scargill had merely been waving at some of his supporters and not making a salute. The print workers refused to print the paper and instead a statement on the front page read:

> Members of all the *Sun* production chapels [union branches] refused to handle the Arthur Scargill picture and major headline on our lead story. The *Sun* has decided, reluctantly, to print the paper without either. (The *Sun*, 15 May 1984.)

The wife of serial killer Peter Sutcliffe won enormous damages from Private Eye *magazine. Workers at the* Sun *newspaper refused to print a cover critical of trade unions.*

1 What problems does the 'right of reply' raise for newspapers and magazines? For television and radio? Would the right of reply make it easier or more difficult to publish articles criticizing people?

2 Can you think of ways to make sueing for libel easier for ordinary people?

3 Should print workers be able to censor what appears in the newspaper for which they work? Is it any different from editors altering or withholding articles in their newspapers?

Censorship in context

As we have seen from the previous chapters, censorship takes many forms and is found almost everywhere. Here is an illustration of how it crosses both national and ideological barriers:

> Did I know, Stephen Vizinczey [a Hungarian writer] said, about the guy who had banned one of his plays in Hungary who had called him in and said it was bad, against the Party? Well, in 1959 he was in Canada making a documentary for the Film Board about the way people faced death. Well, Vizinczey was called to the Ministry of Education which controlled the Film Board and was told that the subject was too depressing and the Board had cancelled the film. And the man who told him was the same person, not the same kind of person, but the same person who in 1956 had told him his play was banned in Hungary. Here Mr Vizinczey was in full yell: 'I said "You! Nothing changes. I run across half the world, I write in another language. And I find you behind another desk." ' And the man laughed too. He also had left during the 1956 revolution and was doing what he was good at, sitting at a desk speaking for some minister . . . (Terry Coleman interviewing Vizinczey, the *Guardian,* 19 August 1988.)

Who do you think should decide what is 'filth' and what is not?

The battle to be able to express thoughts and ideas and to spread information about facts and events has been fought since the earliest days of civilization. Once society began to be organized in a formal way, some people wanted to prevent others having their say.

Today, the fight starts in the classroom. School textbooks, particularly on history, have long been a source of concern for educators worried about what influence their contents may have on schoolchildren. The revival of Christian fundamentalism in the USA has led to a considerable increase in censorship of books and school curricula over the last few years. In Japan, textbooks have to be approved by the education ministry and screened by teams of inspectors before being released to schools. The result according to one history professor, Saburo Ienaga, is:

> that the authorization system constitutes a form of 'thought control' which is implemented by ideologically prejudiced bureaucrats working behind closed doors and thereby violates the constitution. (*Index on Censorship.*)

The same powers that are used in South Africa to ban black leaders from speaking are also used to restrict the activity of the racist AWB.

As part of the *glasnost* (openness) process in the USSR, school textbooks are being rewritten to include events - even atrocities caused by former Soviet leaders like Stalin - which had previously been censored out of history books. Milder forms of censorship, however, have many defenders:

> Censorship can be, has been and is being, in some places used as an instrument of tyranny, in others of stupidity and cowardly evasion of truth. But that does not mean that some regulation of what is publicly disseminated for society at large should be entirely abandoned, difficult as it is to draw the line . . . The idea that man has outgrown the need for restraints and prescriptions for the regulation of his life is the most piteous and dangerous fiction that has ever deluded the human mind. One necessary restraint is to guard man from being exposed to stresses, psychological and moral. (Letter to *The Times*, from the Bishop of Peterborough, 29 July 1970.)

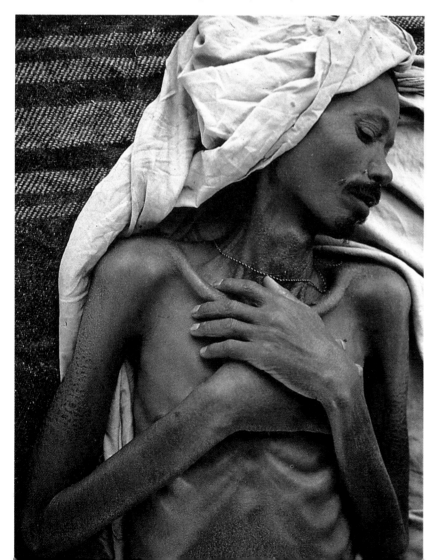

The Ethiopian government's refusal to tell the Ethiopian people about the drought there led to thousands of deaths.

Once the rest of the world knew about the famine, aid began to pour into Ethiopia from other countries. Why did it take so long for them to find out?

While many of the motives of censors may sound reasonable, their work runs counter to one of the very basic freedoms in society - the freedom of expression and information which is one of the cornerstones of all freedoms. One of the most vivid illustrations of its importance comes from this extract about the famine in the mid-1980s in Ethiopia:

> Censorship directly or indirectly contributed to the deaths of tens of thousands of Ethiopians during the three year period I was there. The drought and famine which made headlines in the rest of the world and brought an outpouring of assistance went unreported in the country for at least two years. Actual starvation began to ravage the country as early as 1983. Relief agencies knew it. Many Ethiopian officials knew it, but the government banned any reporting of the oncoming catastrophe in its own media until late 1984.

Although the Ethiopian government did [eventually] allow in foreign reporters so that the outside world would come to its assistance, it deliberately hid the dimensions of starvation from its own public. As explained by the head of the relief agency, the government considered the famine 'an embarrassment and a humiliation to the Revolution'. (Roberta Cohen, 'Censorship Costs Lives', *Index on Censorship*, 1987.)

While not all issues raised by censorship are such matters of life and death, any censor must be able to show that they have a good reason for carrying out their work. Otherwise, their first duty should be to ensure freedom of expression.

1 Why are school textbooks such an obvious target for censors?

2 Why do you think the Ethiopian government was worried about news of the famine leaking out to the outside world? Do governments have the right to withhold information from the people they represent if it will harm their interests?

Glossary

Apartheid: The system of government in South Africa, which denies black people basic human rights because of their skin colour.

Archaic: So old fashioned as to be out of date.

Arrogance: The belief that you are always right and anyone who disagrees with you must be wrong.

Atheist: A person who denies that gods exist.

Broadsheet newspaper: A large newspaper, twice the size of smaller, tabloid ones. They are usually associated with less biased and sensationalist reporting.

Concoct: Make up or invent.

Consensus: A general agreement among the majority of people.

Darwinism: Charles Darwin's theory that people are evolved from animals, which most scientists now accept.

Disseminate: Spread around. The word is normally used when talking about information in a written form.

Dub: Add sound that was recorded separately to a piece of film.

Enmity: Very strong dislike or hatred.

Exorbitant: So big or high as to seem unfair.

Expedient: To someone's advantage. An expedient act may not be moral, but it is usually profitable in some way.

Falklands: Islands off the coast of Argentina which both the UK and Argentina claim to own. The two countries fought a war there in 1982.

Fundamentalism: The belief that everything a religion says is fact and unquestionable.

Glasnost: The process in the USSR which means that events that had been proscribed can now be discussed in the open.

Heretic: A person who refuses to accept orthodox religious views.

Humanist: Someone who believes that only people have control over how their lives turn out.

Ideology: The group of ideas that is drawn on to make a political viewpoint.

Imminent: About to happen.

Legitimate: In accordance with the law.

Mainstream: The prevailing view, which most people in society are willing to go along with.

Malvinas: The Argentine name for the group of islands known in the UK as the Falklands.

Modicum: A very small amount.

Orthodox: Normal and accepted, especially when talking about religion.

Pacifist: Someone who refuses to fight in a war because of the conviction that all wars are wrong.

Perspective: A mental or physical point of view.

Prejudice: An unfair opinion formed without any reason or evidence.

Proscribe: Reject something, claiming it to be dangerous and forbidding it to be seen.

Racism: Unpleasant or violent behaviour towards members of another race.

Repression: Controlling, using effort or force.

Scurrilous: Insulting language, sometimes in a half serious, half playful way.

Sinn Fein: A political party in Northern Ireland that has strong links with the Irish Republican Army.

Suppression: Withholding or withdrawing from publication.

Further reading

Amnesty International, *Amnesty International Report* (annual).

Article 19 is responsible for many publications, among them *Information, Freedom and Censorship*, edited by Kevin Boyle; details of other books are available on application (see address in further information).

Roger Bolton, *Death on the Rock and other stories*, WH Allen/Hoptomen, 1990.

Gail Chester & Julienne Dickey (eds.), *Feminism and Censorship*, Prism Press.

Donna A Demac, *Liberty Denied: the current rise of censorship in the USA*, Pan American Center, 1989.

Paul O'Higgins, *Censorship in Britain*, Nelson.

Junction Books, *Offensive Literature*, 1982.

Index on Censorship is responsible for many books, among them *Freedom to Publish* by Peter Calvocoressi; details of other publications are available on application (see address in further information).

P Sieghart, *The International Law of Human Rights*, Clarendon Press, and (ed) *Human Rights in the UK*, Pinter Publishers Ltd, 1988.

Des Wilson, *The Secrets File*, Heinemann, 1984.

Further information

Australia

Amnesty International, Victoria Branch, PO Box 1333, Richmond N, Victoria 2121.

Canada

Amnesty International, English-speaking Section, 130 Slater Street, Suite 900, Ottawa, Ontario KIP 6ET.

New Zealand

New Zealand Council for Civil Liberties, PO Box 337, Wellington.

UK

Amnesty International, 5 Roberts Place, Bowling Green Lane, London EC1 0EJ.

Article 19, 90 Borough High Street, London SE1.

Index on Censorship, 39c Highbury Place, London N5 1QP.

USA

Committee to Protect Journalists, 16 East 42nd Street, 3rd Floor, New York, NY 10017.

The Reporters Committee for Freedom of the Press, Suite 504, 1735 Eye Street NW, Washington, DC 20006.

Acknowledgements

The publishers gratefully acknowledge permission from the following to reproduce copyright material: Amnesty International for an extract from the Education Project on *Censorship*; Article 19 for extracts from *World Report 1988* and 'Censorship and its History' by Michael Scammell; Ballantine for extracts from *Dangerous Dossiers* by Herbert Mitgang; Terry Coleman for an extract from his interview with Stephen Vizinczey; *Congressional Quarterly* for an extract from 'Mass Media and American Politics' by Doris Graber; Greenpeace for an extract from *Greenpeace;* the *Guardian* for extracts from an article by Tony Benn on 7 April 1989 and a quotation of Sam Chugg on 15 February 1990; the *Independent Magazine* for extracts concerning wartime propaganda on 2 October 1990; Index on Censorship for contributions to their journal by Jim Campbell, John Lloyd, Saburo Ienaga and Roberta Cohen, MacMillan for extracts from *The Press in Wartime* by Sir Edward Cook, *The Media and the Falklands Campaign* by Valerie Adams and *Glasnost in Britain* by Norman Buchan and Tricia Sumner; the National Council for Civil Liberties for an extract from 'Section 28' by Madeleine Colvin; *The New Statesman* for an extract from 'Mrs Mary Whitehouse's Private Member' by Joan Smith; the *New York Times* for extracts from 'Why We Should Change the Libel Law' by Floyd Abrahams and an article by James Renton; Penguin for extracts from *Freedom, the Individual and the Law* by Geoffrey Robertson; Prism Press for an extract from *Feminism and Censorship* by Gail Chester and Julienne Dickey; Sage for extracts from *Journalists at War* by David Morrison and Howard Tumler; the *Sun* for quotation of their front page; *The Sunday Times* for an extract concerning horror videos; *The Daily Telegraph* for an extract from an article by John Birt; *The Times* for extracts from letters from Roald Dahl and the Bishop of Peterborough; *The Witness* for an extract from 'Does the US Have a Free Press?' by Michael Parenti; *Woman* magazine for a quotation of Sam Fox.

The publishers would like to thank the following for providing illustrations for this book: Allsport 38; David Bowden 28; J Allan Cash 9 (top), 27; Chapel Studios 32, 45; Eye Ubiquitous 12; Joel Finler 14; John Frost 14 (bottom), 41; Gay Times 31 (bottom) (Bill Short); Kobal Collection 6, 33, 34, 36; Living Marxism *cover*, 4, 26 (Simon Norfolk), 13 (Pandora Anderson), 15 (David Rourke); Network 9 (bottom), 42 (Paul Lowe), 44 (Goldwater); Photri 7, 30 (top); Private Eye 39; Rex Features 16, 31 (top), 35; Clare Short 30 (bottom); Topham/Associated Press 5, 8, 10, 11, 14 (top), 17, 18, 19 (top & bottom), 20, 21, 22, 23, 25, 29 (top & bottom), 40, 43 (top & bottom); Wayland 37 (Tim Woodcock).

Index

Page numbers in **bold** may refer to both illustrations and text. Others refer to text alone.

American Civil War, censorship in 18
Australia **10**

blasphemy 23-6
Board of Film Classification (UK) 35-6
business interest and
    ownership of media 15-16

Canada 42
'censor', origin of word 5
censorship, definition of 4-5
Christianity and blasphemy laws **23-5**
Church, role of the 6
Crimean War 17

Darwinism, censorship of **22**
defamation 38-41

Ethiopia, media censorship in **44, 45**
European Court of Human Rights 38

Falklands War, censorship in the **17,**
    18, 20
film censorship 20, **33**
    classification 35
First Amendment, US Constitution 13
First World War 18, 21
Fox, Samantha **31**
Freedom of Information Act
    (USA) 12-13

Grenada, invasion of **18, 20**, 21

history and censorship 43-4
homosexuality and censorship **31-2**

index of banned books 6
Inquisition 6

Japan, censorship of textbooks in 43

Kirkup, James, blasphemy trial 23

Lawrence, DH and censorship
    of novels 28, **29**
libel **38-41**

literature, censorship of 29, 32

Maxwell, Robert **14, 39**
media, ownership of the 14-16
Murdoch, Rupert 14
Muslims and blasphemy law 25

New Nation 9
Northern Ireland 4, 10, **12, 13**

obscenity 27-37
ownership and censorship **14-16**
political censorship **7**, 8-13
pornography **28**, 29-31
Press Council (UK) 40
Production Code Administration
    (USA) and film censorship 33-5

religious views, censorship of 6, 22-5
Roman Empire 6
Romania, political censorship in **8**-9
Rushdie, Salman **4**, 6, 24-6
Russell, William Howard 17

Satanic Verses **23, 24, 26, 42**
Scargill, Arthur 41
Second World War 20
Section 28 31-2
Short, Clare **30**-31
Sinn Fein, broadcasting ban on 10, 12
Sisulu, Zwelakhe 9
South Africa, political censorship in
    9, 43
Spanish Inquisition **6**
Spycatcher, banning of **10-11**, 29
Sun (newspaper)
    and libel 41
    and pornography 30-31
Switzerland, religious censorship in 25

Taylor, John and blasphemy 23
television censorship 33-7
trade unions and

newspaper censorship 41
UK
    censorship 7
    concentration of media
        ownership 14-15
    Falklands War 18, 20
    film censorship **35-7**
    freedom of information or
        expression laws, lack of 10-12
    homosexuality 31-2
    libel 40-41
    obscenity trials 29
    pornography 30-31
    television censorship 37
    Video Recording Act 36-7
USA
    book publishing 15
    business interests and
        censorship 15-16
    Civil War 18
    Darwinism censored **22**
    film censorship 33-5
    First Amendment 13
    First World War 21
    Freedom of Information Act 12-13
    invasion of Grenada 21
    McCarthy **21**
    ownership of media 14-16
    religious censorship 22
    school books and
        curricula censored 43
    Vietnam War 18, **19**
USSR 44

Video Recording Act (UK) 36-7
Vietnam War, censorship in 18
violence, on television and videos
    35-7

war, censorship and 17-21
West Germany and libel 40

CAT.
N.O

O ... HO ITY